GW00393590

STOLEN MOMENTS

poetry pt today

Stolen Moments

Edited by Suzy Walton

First published in Great Britain in 2001 by Poetry Today, an imprint of
Penhaligon Page Ltd, Remus House, Coltsfoot Drive, Woodston, Peterborough. PE2 9JX

A Catalogue record for this book is available from the British Library

ISBN 1 86226 603 4

Typesetting and layout, Penhaligon Page Ltd, England.
Printed and bound by Forward Press Ltd, England

Foreword

Stolen Moments is a compilation of poetry, featuring some of our finest poets. This book gives an insight into the essence of modern living and deals with the reality of life today. We think we have created an anthology with a universal appeal.

There are many technical aspects to the writing of poetry and *Stolen Moments* contains free verse and examples of more structured work from a wealth of talented poets.

Poetry is a coat of many colours. Today's poets write in a limitless array of styles: traditional rhyming poetry is as alive and kicking today as modern free verse. Language ranges from easily accessible to intricate and elusive.

Poems have a lot to offer in our fast-paced 'instant' world. Reading poems gives us an opportunity to sit back and explore ourselves and the world around us.

Contents

Safety First

I launched the NASA Space Shuttle ~ that is,
I launched the meeting that launched the ideas
that launched the plans that launched the hardware
that launched the Shuttle. Till then, the Shuttle was
but a gleam in NASA's eye. The meeting introduced
the bride and groom; NASA outlined its needs,
and suppliers went home to work up proposals.

All went well till the meeting's third day,
when the hundreds of people looked forward
to a picnic lunch on our grassy grounds instead of
in our plain-Jane cafeteria ~ weather permitting.
Late that morning torrents of rain suddenly
threatened. No one had rain gear. Disaster loomed.
As manager of the conference, the decision
on indoors versus outdoors was mine, underlined
by my having quoted Napoleon to the gathering:
One bad general is better than two good ones.
I waited as long as I dared, then opted for indoors.
It did not rain. But Safety First had been at stake.

Looking back, I wish I had chosen outdoors,
it had rained hard, and all had been drenched.
This is not my being sadistic ~ on the contrary,
then some chances might not have been taken
on programs that ran into troubles. Safety First!
In the Safety First slogan, remember who came in
second and third? Safety ~ for win, place and show!

Roger Mather

Killing Fields

Funeral pyres, smouldering through the night.
Across the land, the smell of burning flesh.
Empty fields, no sheep or cattle to be seen.
Foot and mouth, again, ravishing the land.

Farmers and smallholders, their livelihood, drifting in the wind.
The end for many, but some will start again.
The countryside is closed, the public, must keep out.
Must contain the disease, roadblocks, are put up.

People with placards, shouting their disgust.
Men in white overalls, faces covered with masks.
Shooting and killing, in fields close to home.
Buried time bombs, what will the future hold?

Wayne Cotter

Lost And Found God

I felt as though I were lost for a moment,
A sensation of insecurity
The chaos of life brings turmoil to the innermost self
Then calmness came like a light out of the blue,
A certain feeling. That all will be well,
Peace came when I realised we are but human,

Do your best, then leave your cares in God's hands
Being of divine source, all understanding
And loving in so many ways,
We must stop ~ accept what is, and be at peace,
Knowing that God's love is within each one.

Eleanor Haydon Sanderson

Nicetown-On-Sea (Padstow)

Blackbirds at my beckoning.
Dotterels at my feet.
Softly spoken Cornish voices,
Wafting through the street.

Boats. My god so many!
Colour. My god surprise!
Winding road a precipice,
Drops me off at paradise.

Hostelries. What welcome!
Nectar from their pumps.
Glowing ambience from within,
Hey! I've come up trumps.

And endless row of benches,
Each one bears a plaque.
Strange to think memorials,
Soothe my aching back.

Soaring skylarks.
Friendly dogs.
(Their master throws them sticks.)
March winds blow a soothing song,
(Still time to learn new tricks!)

Now the tidal climax.
The sandbar disappears.
Boats glide out majestically.
Minus all the cheers.

Why can't *all* towns be like this?
Example to us all.
Nature blends with will of man,
And happy memories never pall.

And a few lines after a tiring visit to Clovelly.
Cobbles.

Cobbles, cobbles, everywhere.
Precipitous or what!
All this effort, just to view,
One, worn out. Lobster pot.

J E Chambers

To Dream A Promise

A dream is a promise you can make for yourself
A promise is not to be left on the shelf,
You must wait till the time is right for you
To make your promise, a dream come true.

You must work at your promise, every day
Not letting obstacles get in the way,
It is you that makes the life that you lead
Wait awhile, it will put you in good stead.

Don't be in a hurry to run through your life
For you may stumble and cause some strife,
Don't turn your back on the sick and the poor
Don't hide away and close the door.

Remember that charity, begins at home
Not to love, you will always be alone,
So remember that promise you made long ago
To achieve it be patient, and take it slow.

One day that promise will be yours to behold
But it may not be until, you are very old,
Your reward for your dream will be worth the wait
So get on with your life now, don't hesitate.

Jean-Ruth

Sometimes

Sometimes a picture takes my eye
So rare I cannot pass it by,
Dew shining on a spider's web,
Sparkling jewels some sprite has shed.
A shaft of light through shady leaves.
A halo round a primrose weaves,
Bluebells on a forest floor
Spring's magic carpet blooms once more.
Sometimes a sound will catch my ear,
Church bells ringing, faint yet clear
Or music with a haunting strain.
You hear but once, and ne'er again.
A violin plays on your heart strings
Your spirit soars on angel wings,
You're joyful though part of you is sad,
Yet for that sorrow, you are glad.
Sometimes I'll smell a thing so fair
It lingers on the strangest air
The scent of rain on velvet bloom,
Of roses in the Month of June,
The smell of woodsmoke in a dell
That even summer showers can't quell
Or tangy spray on rocky shore
That fills your senses more and more.
Sometimes a thing will touch my heart,
When did it end? How did it start?
The strangest feeling saps my will
As all at once the earth stands still.
Then something seems to fill my soul,
And now my being is a whole.

B G Metcalfe

The Freedom That Is Ours

Come share the life I love, with me
We'll roam the fields together
At night with the moon and stars above
We'll lie and sleep in the heather.

We'll thank God by day for the sunshine
The birds, the trees and the flowers
And thank Him for His greatest gift
The freedom that is ours.

All the wealth we need, as we stroll along
Is there, by the wayside to see
Everything nature possesses is ours
For all nature lovers it's free.

Where would we be without freedom?
We need to be completely at ease
Free to be bold, like the nomads of old
And rest our heads wheresoever we please.

There's one pleasing thing about freedom
Being able to do our part
In keeping the highways open
For all, with a wanderer's heart.

David Livingstone

Hold Me Now

Here with my head up in the clouds,
I feel I'm spinning around.
Dreams will come and go,
But this is here to stay,
So forever this way.
Hold me now, hold me now,
And say the things you say,
Hold me now, hold me now,
I pray.
So here we are, at the start of this road,
Together building castles in the air.
Words we don't need,
Without you I don't breathe,
Forever building castles in the air.

Hold me now, hold me now,
And say the things you say,
Hold me now, hold me now,
I pray.
So softly like a sigh,
See where the white horses ride,
It all seems so real,
A feeling deep inside,
So our time will go on.
Hold me now, hold me now,
And say the things you say,
Hold me now, hold me now,
I pray.

Clare Sellwood

Jenny (Memories)

Where have you gone?
May I come with you?
Are there fairies there as well?
Is it like a dingly dell?

I hope it isn't dark at night
I hope that you aren't scared.
I think of you a lot you know
Please tell me that it isn't so.

I hold your hand in my mind.
I reach to touch your hair.
I find it so hard to accept
That you are no longer there.

We used to sit and read at night
You used to laugh and say
'Daddy, where do the fairies go
When they fly away?'

I often couldn't answer
I didn't know myself.
Why is it all the hardest things
You have to find within yourself?

Why did she die?
What did I do?
I can't help but blame myself
For not dying too.

She used to skip and laugh with glee
Or watch her films with me.
We sat closely together
Jenny silently on my knee.

I can hear her little voice
Calling me at night
I sometimes run into her room
And expect to find her there.

Why am I having such trouble
Accepting that she has gone?
My little ray of sunshine
Someone else has won.

Annie M Rawsthorne

Not Revealed To Us

Starting boldly on the upward path,
We trod our hopeful way
Towards seeing the one-off temple:
A sight we'd heard our efforts would repay.
Then, after seeing the rarest of shrubs
And breathing their mystic perfume.
Then too sitting resting a bit beside a lake
In whose murky depths the full, fat, wriggling trout
Swam, cooled from the big sun's bake,
Bloated and content, in their spumied water pent.
We, in due time, on and on went and went and went
And, as you've guessed, we never met old Nidden's temple.
Later, we discovered in conversation, it was a tough test,
Of wind and truly aged, burnt-out arthritic limb
To climb and climb and climb the rugged other path
In order to pay respects to her or him.
Never mind, apart from this one kinky-boo,
We enjoyed ourselves and used our cameras wisely too.

Ruth Bibby

Life

Life is like a jigsaw, and it's very hard to place,
All the bits and pieces into their allotted space,
So often we realise how things would have been,
If into the future we could have foreseen

Troubles *never* come singly, and that's a fact,
Leaving us puzzled as to how we should act,
But in spite of all the ups and downs,
Smiles and tears, and many frowns,
Things often *do* work out for the best,
Especially when put to the acid test.

Life is what *we* make it, although fate may take a hand,
When things don't work out as we originally planned.
But don't keep moaning about your sad lot,
Be very grateful for what you've already got

Not everyone the headlines make
But if you'll only *give* and not always take,
Satisfaction will its own reward bring,
Contentment and happiness surpass everything

E Kathleen Jones

The Lone Farmer

The farmer, with eyes,
practiced in distant sights
alert to respond for any change
trained after hard-fought rights.

The vixen's feathered trail
of killing for no reason
in common with feline play.

Like war games to leaders
of cults and careers
with feet rooted in clay
stirruped by Pegasus display.

Each season stamped
by the rotation of decay
with creation fulfilled.

The policy of cull in fields
where the animals cowered
senseless and defenceless
against the holocaust
of hate and envy born
of God's laughter
at people who plan.

The farmer's eyes reflected
the full lipped mouth turning
a grin into laughter
at the satisfaction of being
~ a woman being.

Michael A Fenton

The Tower Of Time

The tall, tall Tower of Time appears to be
more fragile the closer to its base you try to go.
The hazy indistinct foundations are made frail
by loss of memory and the passing years.
The past all fractured through. The stairways
although clear, have steps that grow more tatty
and with broken treads
the further back you go from here and now.

The closer to the present, the tower's structures sturdier seem.
The present, pristine new, with fresh built thought agleam.
Above the present time, the edifice is naught, a blank.
No matter how the architects will strive
with their blue-prints, imaginative plans ~ and new ideas alive,
the Tower of Time will not grow by a single fraction of an hour
until the present forms the past and becomes
the topmost layer of the slowly rising tower
As the silent clock of life ticks inexorably on.

D G W Garde

Suspended In Time

My thoughts rise into the air.
Winging their way upwards and onwards
Into the atmosphere.

I listen to the voice of the wind
As it calls to the sea.
And the song of the waves as they roll towards me
Mingled with sighs of lost souls from the deep
Pebbles flung in their wake.

So calm your wrath Oh sea.
Lest you disturb dreams of souls
Who sleep the long sleep.

Slowly the moon will rise
Casting paths of light across your great divide.
Her beauty through sea mist to shine
And beams like fingers point the way
For passing ships this night.

Many centuries have gone.
Once I was here in another form
Now I stand my soul encased
Until time erodes
A Rock.

Margaret H Mustoe

June 7th 2001 ~ General Election Battle Song

What have they got?
That Scottish lot,
Besides, haggis and the kilt,
Ben Nevis on high,
Nearly touching the sky,
Hadrian's Wall should never been built.

What have they got?
That foreign Welsh lot,
Besides pancakes and many castles,
Snowdonia on high,
Nearly touching the sky,
And a language you can't use on parcels.

What have they got?
That green Irish lot,
Besides Guinness and lucky 4-leaf clover,
Of Blarney in Cork,
Gifts of eloquence and talk,
And Irish whiskey to make you fall over.

The English have got,
What others have not,
A language the world's understanding,
Sophisticated and true,
Not misled by the few,
A rich country we all have a hand in.

So, where ere you live,
Your vote you should give,
To the political party that pleases,
Be it Lib Dem or Tory,
Or New Labour for *glory*,
On June 7th, your conscience, it eases.

John Harper-Smith

Sink Estate

Slums and scum-bags,
Burglars and toe-rags,
Inner-city dilapidation equals degenerating civilisation,
Rigid steel shutters repel you with ease,
Obscene graffiti gratuitously greets you,
Flaking red paint compounds neurotics feeling faint,
Nuisance neighbours don't do any favours,
Kindness and courtesy perceived as weakness.
Just sink or swim on something that's grim,
Shackled mongrels bark endless annoyance,
Dipso boozers clash with smack-head losers and just trash it!
Self-service shoplifters on their rounds daily,
Violence and filth swagger down main streets,
Stolen jam-jars taunt frustrated police cars,
Frightened grandma's, locked behind bars,
Neighbourhood watch, kicked in the crotch,
Back to front wasters breeding more system breakers,
Teenage mobsters unlacing their fashion,
Ex reg and Y reg the limit of their passion,
The scrawl of the pipes will never inspire moronic tradition,
Black lines and white lines, best not to cross them,
Blue lines don't count just knock them right out,
Benefit fraudsters wheeling,
While druggies keep dealing,
Stanley and Maureen,
Mortgaged perennials trapped in the mire,
How do they cope while next door is on fire?
Festering malady on a contemporary estate,
Such is sink fate,
How great is the waste in this noxious place.

Robert Henry Lonsdale

Watching

Sitting on the doorstep looking out,
and everything is looking fine.
Birds singing as loud as they can,
clothes pegs hanging from the line.

Rooftops sloping downwards,
towards the garden shed.
Butterflies and bees,
flying around the flower bed.

Sunshine shining brightly,
as people mow the grass.
Children's toys lying around,
cracks appearing in the path.

Fences dividing the gardens,
from us and next door.
People lying in the sun,
they will get burned that's for sure.

Television aerials,
appearing in the sky line.
As I sit here on my doorstep,
everything is looking fine.

John Barr

A Plant

I had a plant once,
a miniature tree with buds of luxurious green.
I nurtured this plant, fed it every part of me.
Those leaves fanning into an effervescent dome
was a beauty I admired.

But suddenly, one morning, nothing.
Its stalk uncovered ~
on the floor scattered leaves lay in disarray.

Sad memories unrolled before my eyes,
couldn't they hear my cries,
my forgiveness,
yearning for all those bitter wasted years . . .

I had a mother once,
a miniature woman shrouded in sadness.
I didn't nurture this mother ~
too many arguments soiled our earth.
When her body wilted into a skeletal frame I walked away.

And suddenly one morning, nothing.
On the floor she lay,
pills scattered by her side.

My plant has now regained a few speckled leaves.
With a grain of care
I have brought a glimpse of vigour back into its soul.

Unfortunately I cannot bring my mother back.
Guilt parcels itself deep inside me,
and every day I mourn for the growth we never shared.

Sally Ann Ling

The Wind

Where does it come from?
Where does it go?
I've read all the theories
But does anyone really know?
In winter, we fill every nook and cranny,
To keep its icy blast at bay
In summer we uncover as much as we dare.
'Please come blow over me today.'
It moans in the chimneys,
Like souls from the grave.
It carries great waters,
Building up mountainous waves.
It comes in gentle zephyrs,
Rippling waves in fields of corn
Making even the hottest day ~ bearable ~
Like the breeze that comes with the dawn.
So ~ in winter ~ pull your warm coat closer
Bravely ~ battle against every blast
The wind when it has blown its fury out,
Will be gentle ~ kind ~ and welcome at last.
Wind ~ where do you come from?
I really do not know,
But with temperatures in the 80°s today,
Please touch me before you go.

I M Spencer

One Summer's Day

I took a stroll one summer's day
Over the hills not far away,
As I walked the road thro' Tatenhill
Not a soul I passed, I came upon an
Ancient well, a relic from the past.
I climbed a stile and wandered across the hills
So steep I was followed by a large flock
Of woolly coated sheep.
I rambled thro' the green woods and there
Before my eyes a stunning view of Burton
Expanding now in size, as I gazed upon the
Scene below, the heat was so intense
It caused a shimmering misty glow upon the
Valley spread below.

This walk that I had taken I began to reminisce
'Twas on these hills one summer's day I pledged
My life to one man and sealed with a kiss
But now alone I wander along life's busy path
Recalling precious moments from my life
That's swiftly passed.

E Brooks

Scorned Love

You scorned the love I gave to you
And threw that love away
But perhaps sometimes in the future
You will come to rue that day

For true love might come just once
And could be here to stay
But if it is neglected
That love could die away

But if it is cherished
It will grow stronger day by day
And overcome any obstacles
That could come its way.

Diana Daley

Moccasin Telegraph

The Queen's head the crown
bull and the harvester
fire storms and shadows
in the urban metropolis,

Nights dented sprawl
cascading in the valley
car diamond necklaces
a mirror for the past,

Swiss automatic
twenty-three jewels
water resistant
genuine leather,

Invention says I'm late
love phones, must artic'ulate
while we charge along
chariots phosphor bronze,

Soft gentle speech
again to meet
that seventy miles an hour
give us another hour,

We then harvest time
our pursuit to dream
of elysium together
the past behind us.

Jeremy Jones

The Shepherdess

This beautiful young maiden captured behind a pane of glass
The lovely sweet shepherdess from a distant ageless past
Those rounded cheeks and those smiling lips were like blushing rose
There I stared and admired that simple loveliness of her pose

Those painted slender hands held a tiny lamb with tender care
There was a white bonnet gently covered her flowing red hair
Those beautiful smiling eyes were so blue like a cloudless summer sky
Then I swore her kissable young mouth let out a silent sigh

This young shepherdess beauty has frozen her girlish charm will
never age
Those painted bygone years has allowed us to turn its ageless page
There I stood before her I lovingly could not take my eyes from
her face
My heart was held spellbound by the beauty of her charming grace

There was a small tear this striking portrait will never be mine
to hold
My heart stood still when I found my lovely shepherdess had
been sold
That charming young maiden her ageless beauty I will never
again find
The deep longing I have for her will stay forever in my sadden mind

This beautiful young shepherdess will hang and adorn a rich
man's hall
This priceless beauty hangs like a prisoner on an oak covered wall
I never forget that remarkable painting behind a golden frame
This wonderful portrait the shepherdess that became her single name

John F Grainger

I Wandered

I wandered lonely in a crowd
Spying faces as I see
Always in depressions shroud
I see them do they see me
So think of me as you glance
With fleeting eyes that meet by chance

Often though I walk and pass
Catching eyes with vacant stare
Never even think to ask
Without so much as any care
Do any really feel as low
As we pass they come and go

Lonely in each crowded street
Passing all those aching hearts
Rarely though by chance to meet
Those who live in same parts
Lonely faces all askew
Can't I start my life anew

Raymond Peter Walker

Shy

Do you fully understand what it's like to be shy
To wish the ground would swallow you up,
To sometimes just wish you could die,
To be so crippled with fear
You never live life to the full,
To just sit alone and cry and cry,
To ask yourself why,
To always feel as if you're being watched,
When really you are not
To never be able to feel at ease,
And always be eager to please,
To always feel the odd one out,
To always have that self doubt.

Danielle Gallagher

The Killing Fields

I watch the way that man destroys and see the effect on little boys,
the children that from him will learn how to condemn and kill
then burn.
To stop the spread of an old disease when known injections would
appease,
and not to learn from the past how long their damage here could last.
With skies of smoke and acrid fume and a way of life is turned
to doom,
their years of work and money spent by those who own and some
who rent.
It seems as if they now don't care as even the healthy they
won't spare,
at this time of spring and new born life God help the farmer and
his wife.

The last nine weeks we have watched the spread and the stacking of
the piles of dead,
if what the experts say is true the infection spread is halfway
through.
But to sit in London far away and watch the problem where others
stay,
as they struggle to survive and wait for compensation to arrive.
This money that will not replace the stock you lost or the grief you
faced,
for now it will become a race for farmers with stock to replace.
And of course this will be at a price for those supplying very nice,
but for many far too late just a for sale sign on the gate.

D S Joyce

First Loss Of Innocence

Oh how and why that fateful night,
When she was taken from my sight.
Stolen from her caring arm,
Delivered into storming harm.
Will I be yet gifted an earnest return,
To the love that my heart doth yearn.
Oh innocence, what a splendid ill,
To be divorced, estranged against my will.

Scott Lyons

The Boundless

Does the dark actually exist?
Or is it just the absence of light
That deceives the eye, which inspires feelings
Out of Mind and Sight
Or is this mystery an illusion
Magical?
Which makes all things tangible disappear
With no regards for joy or fear

To perceive the mind must be stretched
Beyond imagination
For this will prevent elimination
Of the boundless the source of all
Which as and will always exist
For nothing comes from nothing
A fact only the cynical will resist

Moreover reason states
That a billion times nothing
Leaves nothing to embrace
Therefore something both mutable and eternal must exist
Within this boundless immortal space
Although imperceptible be that as it may
Its prime mover will be discovered one day

So
Older than the world
Before the stars
Creator of all planets
The Moon and the Sun
This is the soil from which all life begun

David O'Pearce

It'll All End In Tears

She was knockin' back the vodka like there was no tomorrow
Everybody said she'll bring you nothing but sorrow
Yet for her you would beg, steal or borrow
And she'll bring you nothing but tears in the end

So tired running round in circles, still I've never done enough
All fired up, you're gonna make it, right up to the top
You've got your foot on the pedal, but you've got no brakes to stop
It'll bring you nothing but tears in the end

Now they've got you surrounded but there's nothing left to defend
And the water is rising on ever shrinking land
And you know your heart is broken, but you know it'll never mend
She'll bring you nothing but tears in the end

She'll bring you nothing but tears in the end
You can run, you can hide, but you just can't pretend
She'll bring you nothing trouble my friend
She'll bring you nothing but tears in the end.

Richard Gilpin

First Love, Last Love

You quietly asked that Death would let you wait
Till I had put my infant in your arms:
You, in your Northern gloaming, fading fast,
Left my new blossom, fragile, in my arms.

But Death, who had not looked upon my last love
Untimely seized my first love, pain ~ purged, pure.
Locked in the anguished joy of childbirth
I could not bring my tender gift to you.

But so it is in life's regeneration:
The oldest is reshaped to make the new
We hold the violet's very tender blue,
Believe that every Winter ends in Spring.

I see my old love by both wind and water
Where bluebells tangle with the sea-blown thrift:
While Nature knows perpetual renewal
This trinity of love can conquer Death.

Irene Cook

On The Death Of My Husband

Damp, sweaty sheets, feverish brow,
Eyes stabbed by the light ~
We'll use candlelight now.

I hold your hand gently,
I keep my voice low,
There's so much to say, Love,
Before you let go.

We have much to remember
Down the years we have shared,
Children and laughter
And joy uncompared.

There's been sadness and sorrow
But our love has been true,
We've faced problems together
And always won through.

And now you are drifting,
You've nothing to fear,
Your pain will soon vanish,
Angel wings hover near ~

In the midst of this anguish,
I ask You, 'Lord, why?'

But ask not who is dying, Love,
I know that it is I.

Jane Finlayson

Haunted
(To GW)

The fifth of May, the magic day
On which we met with instant love;
Its fortieth anniversary has sadly come and gone.

Mercifully, I cannot now recall
The day on which our romance met its end;
Although I know with certitude the place,
And the sultry summer evening
Which the gods saw fit to send.

Did someone say that heartaches cannot last?
Much more in love than I knew at the time,
I thought the lovely episode was firmly in the past;
But I was wrong:
The past, with all its consequence,
Is part of here and now,
And never ever leaves us.

Whom did she marry? Is she happy?
And does she ever think of me?
How I wish I knew!
Forty years have passed, it's true;
Nevertheless, I wish I knew.
Alas, the final die is cast;
Did someone say that heartaches cannot last?

Edward Francis

Heart For Sale

Georgie Porgie pudding and pie,
Kissed the girls on the sly,
But unlike Georgie
I don't want to partake in some wild orgy,
The only tale I have to regale,
Is simply that of a heart for sale,
On it's a note,
On it is wrote,
I'm a little old fashioned,
When it comes to passion,
I like an old-fashioned waltz,
I believe in love at first sight,
And all sentimental schmaltz,
And the moon by night,
I will send you a Fabergé Egg in gold ormolu,
To celebrate a love forever true,
Only the best will do,
Engraved upon it is 'I love you'
Send you Cushat doves that coo,
Cheer you up when you are blue,
Georgie Porgie pudding and pie,
Kissed the girls and made them cry,
But I don't want you to weep
Or a love that's going cheap
I dream of you when I'm asleep.
I only have one heart for sale,
So like a cowboy following the trail,
I keep my heart in a casket,
So I say with glee,
Be kind to me,
Don't ask it.

Alan Pow

Ode To Love

My parents ask you to my house for tea
but use a language of antiquity.
You are so young and talking disappears
but passion stays to keep away our tears.

Our eyes are telling of those days of love
when hungry kisses and my hands above
your trembling breast showed us the certainty
of passion and a lifelong purity.

My mood was madcap, frantic and bizarre
but now I see you as a shining star.
When sailing in a ship from night to day
I know your life will show me on my way.

I do not need you here when I can see
the sort of person who I want to be.
I see tall mountains which I need to climb
so we must part until another time.

I move from our romance with innocence
still seeking for a life of affluence.
I love you more than ever in my heart
but looking forward means that we must part.

Nancy Reeves

Let It Be Me

Silence.
Silently I watch.
I switch my love
From one to the other of you,
But I wear not my heart on my sleeve.

I have watched one of you adore me
Shower me with treats and kisses,
Your love so great, it is enough
To suffocate me.
But I saw you being carried away,
Never to return.

Another of you loved me, at the same time,
Detesting me.
I never knew what to make of your love ~
Unpredictable as it was.
But I saw you being carried away,
Never to return.

Now I never know what to think
Of the three that are left to me.
One I will follow to the end of the earth
One pities me, I know not why,
And one to which I could never lie.

These three I trust, yet could never love.
I dare not truly give my heart again
Because, dog though I am, I could not stand
The pain of seeing my owners leave.

To see any more owners leave
To see them carried away,
Never to return.

Next time, love return, and let it be me who is taken away.

Anne Hayes (13)

Out Of The Blue

Years of pain
Of angst and doubt
Anxiety and depression
Were blown away
One day
When out of the blue
She pierced my heart
Her smile beguiled me
Her deep pools of hazel eyes belied her innocence
And now I lie awake
Each eternal night
Alone in darkness
Penning poems
Which cannot do justice to
My feelings
For her loveliness is a vision
She who came into my life
Out of the blue
Into my heart

Ian Speirs

Ode To Love

How oft I wish I were with thee,
Once more your pretty head incline to me
How oft I dream of thee, contented to draw near,
No reward would I ask of thee,
Just fill my dreams a little longer,
With loving arms around me,
Keeping my tears at bay.
As summer flowers begin to bloom, engage my heart a little longer, bring back
The sparkle within mine eye, filled with a growing passion, when I am with thee . . .
Across the sky with larks I'll fly, they leave me far behind . . .
But you and your memory forsake me never,
From my heart will never fly ~
Love so sweet, as when I am with thee . . .

Liz Dicken

Dale

'I want them.'
'I want them all.'
'I want them all right now.'
'I can't have all this again.'
'I've got to be with it tomorrow.'
'I want them all, out of the way.'
'My eyes have to be dry.'

They were after that.
After something I'd never felt before.
A hopeless letting go.
A 'help me' all alone,
my nose dripping in the sink.
I got them, I got them all.

I suppose you could call it insurance,
insurance for the next day.
The day before Christmas Eve, '93.
I got them, I got them all, almost.

I know what he would have said,
said about my insurance.
'John my dear boy, don't cry for me,
cry for your beloved Man City.'

John Walker

Strange Love

Love comes but once and then perhaps too late
He stood there smiling at his open door
I never had a warning of my fate.

His smile meant I was lost forevermore
My foolish heart began to leap and soar
Love comes but once and then perhaps too late.

He didn't even ask me for a date
I don't expect to see him anymore
I never had a warning of my fate.

I was collecting for the local fete
My tin was heavy and my feet were sore
Love comes but once and then perhaps too late.

I was enchanted on that autumn day
I later heard that he had moved away
I never had a warning of my fate.

In after years no other could replace
The smile that lingered on that stranger's face
Love comes but once and then perhaps too late.

I hoped someone like him would come my way
But there was none who could such charm display
I never had a warning of my fate.

This happened far away and long ago
But time has only made the memory glow
I never had a warning of my fate
Love comes but once and then perhaps too late.

Elsie Karbacz

Ode To Nada

Bright star of love you pitched into my dream.
Proud Nada in the dream's uncertain sphere
Your light it beckoned to me. Did I scream?
No. I to follow blindly had a care.
Trembling my sad lips spoke the lone word 'love'
In answer to your beauty's silent call
As all alone I walked into the night.
A dove of peace? It hovered stark above
The place where love beckoned in the fall
And we two were locked in an embrace tight.

Your life was resurrected in my dream
Your youthful lily's bloom in prime of life
Hidden forever in the dark earth's seam.
There, on so many founts of futile strife,
The good are foiled within life's darker sea.
Nada, your troubled path in death I saw
Through a tight blindfold of sorrowing tears,
Shed piously this flow for all to see.
A diamond's star is born without a flaw
Nurtured in the earth's bosom many years.

Sweet Nada, was the dream a thread of hope?
A dream's live focus is in nature's law
A helpline willing us to cope
Where we might sink inside a black hole's maw.
Eternity was in your pouted lips,
Your honeyed breath it blew a fearful gale.
Life's an eternal dungeon without end
Tho' love's star dreamed may launch a thousand ships.
We two in life and death may now set sail
Anchored in sweet love's tryst our lives to blend.

Angus Richmond

Lost Heart

My heart is aching I miss you so much,
Never again to feel your tender touch,
Never again to look into your eyes so blue,
Or to feel the love I had for you.
Why did you have to go away,
Time could have healed the pain,
I could not beg you to stay,
For I could have lost you again.
Your love was not mine to keep,
Your hand not mine to hold,
When I think of you I sit and weep,
Please come back my love from the cold.
The months go by I try to forget the love I have for you,
I cannot forget those happy times and a love that was so true,
When I am old and grey I will treasure my memories every day,
I will never forget you dear even though you are far away.
My heart is on fire when I think of you,
We had a wonderful love so true,
And as I wake up to face the day without you near,
The future seems very unclear.
The love of my life was by my side,
When you went away I cried and cried,
I must face the future with a smile and a cheer,
And pretend to myself that you are still near.
One day perhaps you will return again,
And help me ease this terrible pain,
But now I am free to love at last
My true love is in the past.

M Stevens

Take Me Down

Take me down so I can forget
I fear I'm ordinary
Just like everyone else

The winner takes all
But the Game is fixed
And I am growing tired of this masquerade
It's getting too hard to tell
Where what I am ends
And what they think of me begins

So now where do we go from here?
We have come a long way from playing in the sand
The tide has come in
And washed our footprints away

I feel hollow
As I struggle to breathe through my wicker exterior
Yet no one may help me
As I fear they will not like what they uncover
That I am not what they expected or indeed what I have claimed to be
And that yes I am ordinary
And destined to live a life of shocking anonymity

Now there is a pill to take
A refuge from the outside world
A place where the sad and restless dwell to waste their time
And down here we're all special

Matthew Hare-Scott

The Tale Of The Ancient Fish

My spirit has surfaced somewhat;
I see the shoreline nearer now,
wondering, with race-memory
how life will be
upon that solid earth;

will muscles grieve,
for fin-weaving water-freedom?
And when at length I strain
to stand upright,
how often after shall I fall?

And what shall I do
when my arms are freed at last
from walking?
Will my hand-made toys then sprawl
across that future world,
and even obdurate rock fall,
to the power of my grasping thumb?

Until, in digital disillusion,
I wrap fingers round
my vertebrated neck, squeeze
and suffocate for lack
of this hostile element,
world of air that even now,
chokes my gills.

Noori Anthony Faraj

Special Gift

This is a very special gift,
The reason it's so special is,
It's just for you from me.

Whenever you are lonely
Or even feeling blue,
You only have to read this gift
To know I think of you.

So keep this gift close to your heart,
It's filled with love inside,
Love that is so special,
Just like you are to me.

Sioux McDonnell

Millennium . . .

I sat and watched the TV
And listened to the news
Of politicians, dreams and visions
Spurting out their views

I read stories in the paper,
Of Mother Nature's rage
Too upset to comprehend
I'd turn another page

I listened to the radio
About a man in East Timor
Who found his family butchered
And scattered on the floor

Now they talk about millennium
And tell us that it's great
Though they seem to overlook the fact
Our world is in a state

Countries shackled to a debt
They know they can't repay
Hunger, war, disease is met
By millions every day

Millennium, millennium
To toast a thousand year
Celebrate, contemplate
Delegate your fear

Did you raise your glass on New Year's Eve
To toast a new day's name
And tell me whilst been happy
Did you feel a sense of shame?

Mark David Mahoney

Relief

The pain has now gone.
It is seeping away
Though my veins.
Red water surrounds me.

I smile ~
Knowing this will kill them,
More than it will me.
They will have to live with this.
I won't.
I will be free!

Song in the background;
Note by the kettle.

Seconds tick away.
They are late.
Typical!
Overtime?

I grow weak,
Hard to hear,
Song grows distant,
I fight sleep.
Straining for key . . .
Key in lock.
Any sign of arrival.
Anything!
I give up

Key turned,
Note read.
Body found . . .

Kathryn Kaupa

Counted

You sleep in a doorway
Because you have no bed,
And suddenly you're wanted,
They want to count your head!

You're at last a statistic
For the census list,
And to be realistic
You must not now be missed!

The enumerator will find you
And ask questions on the night.
Your birthdate and what you do,
But ask nothing of your plight.

If you don't co-operate
You are in breach of the act,
And may be fined a £1000
Which is a fact.

Where would the money come from
Is a question you may ask,
But unless that doorway is your domicile
The enumerator has a pointless task ~

In any case the questions asked
With one or two exceptions,
Are irrelevant for a homeless one,
For a census or elections.

D R Thomas

God's Tapestry Of Love
(Dedicated to my Tom)

We exchanged two lives for one
The day we said I do,
And my greatest pride has always been,
That I am part of you.
Yes, our lives are interwoven
By a thread from God above,
Stitched by the Master Tailor
And embroidered with His love.
For only with His blessing
Is it possible to be,
No longer only you and I,
But, forever, truly, we.
And God has blessed our union,
I see it every day.
It's in your smile and in your eyes
And in your loving way.
For these things are my very life,
Your happiness is mine,
I feel your pain, I share your joys,
As our lives are so entwined.
Whether I think back or look ahead
My greatest peace will be,
There's nothing we can't do together
Because you and I are we.

Thomas-Sally Addison

After The Crash

Burdens, mountains, problems, the lot
I've climbed over them all but I haven't forgot.
I am strong, though sometimes too soft I feel
I can't define what is fake or even what is real.
After the crash I then start to convey
That I wasn't the problem, I was only the prey.
Anger towards my blindness and my trust
Shake it off and move on, well I guess I must.
But still it lives, sits on those cheap back seats
I deny it, look away like a con man cheats.
I know where I belong, I know my place in life
It's with my baby girl, not self-inflicted strife!
I will no longer be the prey or a human lie target
Just a mother to my daughter, my wee starlet.

Mhairi Hamilton

Monet

He was an artist that could paint like a bird sings,
Like a lark or a nightingale at the break of dawning.
His clear and precise images, leaving his mind into yours,
As if it was a song and we all knew the chords.
The colours mixing and blending to make the picture,
A book without words ~ but it's still called literature.
Transporting you into a perfect world, never seen before,
From the poppies in the fields, to the cliffs by the shore.

Suzanne Shepherd

The Tramp

A man,
I gaze at him,
His feet muddy and shoes full of holes,
His trousers torn and in rags,
Patch upon patch,
His jacket like a sack.
Tied with string,
His face like coal.
Sorrowed eyes,
Homeless and hungry.
Sleeping in the cold,
Staring at the stars,
Not knowing if they would live through the night.
No one cares,
No one cares.
Not many notice if he is alive,
His life just carries on, just
Nothing to do,
Nowhere to go,
And no one to care,
No one.

S L Teasdale

Gateways

There's voices, harsh groans,
a slap, a cry of pain,
a sharp intake of breath,
the gateway to life,
is breached.

Reading, writing, arithmetic
trigonometry, English,
qualifications!
The gateway to success,
is preached.

Brown hair, slim waist,
pert bum, a smile,
a quick glance,
the gateway to love,
is unleashed.

Years roll by, kids flee the nest,
anticipation, jubilation,
weariness?
The gateway to retirement
is reached.

Gentle walks, creaking joints,
grandchildren, memories,
St Peter's,
the final gateway,
life is complete.

C Matthews

Darkness Descends

Darkness descends, night closes in, cold
Winds rise as the light fades; shadows
Deepen as the sun sets, silhouettes looming.

Daffodils like a sunset in the West, a fall
Of petals, Autumn leaves lying in pools
Beneath naked branches, winged angels of Paradise.

Until the night is past, day dawns, the sun's
Immortal light rises across the garden,
Crocus flowers opening in the light, I part from you.

I believe that one day the shadow will pass,
In the eternal sunshine death and suffering
Shall pass away like a total eclipse.

One morning we shall look up to see
The sun tip the horizon in brilliance,
The dead will arise and time be forgotten.

Reunited, we who mourn; united, we shall
Stand together on some warm shore overlooking
The tranquil, sunlit sea and death shall be defeated.

Janet Eirwen Smith

The Scientific Arts
(256 divided by 123 = 2.0813008)

Do you know that an abacus is a tool?
No, I don't think that you are a fool.
I'm sure you know how to add and subtract,
Else from your work you would soon be sacked.
I'm even sure you can multiply,
The numbers in many rows do lie.
But have you ever tried to divide,
Two big numbers sat side by side?

Don't try it now, you can do it later.
I'll do it now on my calculator.
The Japanese know the Golden Rule,
Very early, they are taught in school,
How to use Napier's sliding rule.
If you will learn, I could show you how.
After, you will be able to take a bow.
This is one of my little tricks:
Take two hundred and fifty six.
Don't lay it out in little sticks,
Just give your abacus three quick flicks.

Let's try to divide by 123
123 doubled becomes 246.
Double gives two but, then we become stuck
'Cos ten remaining will need some luck.
Keep adding noughts 'ad infinitum'
The answer is almost two point oh eight,
With lots of numbers coming too late,
So just add on 1,3,0,0,8.
Revision
Two fifty six on your abacus,
(Don't worry for you won't need to cuss,
It seems to know a lot of short cuts)
Remove 123 and do it twice.
Two is an answer since it's not thrice.

Place decimal point before the remainder
Since all counters left are a number
Only one counter, which gives us a ten.
123 gives us nought again,
So put on a zero and let's try a hundred,
A thousand will start us seeing red.
123 up to eight we are led.
Two decimal zero eight, we're not late.
Sixteen remaining becomes 160
123 once up to 1 we are led.
With any remainder just count 123
And keep adding noughts 'ad infinitum'.

Kristyna Zdrojkowska

What's The Day?

I can't believe tomorrow's Sunday,
A whole half a day, to spend with you,
I can't believe tomorrow's Sunday,
Better get ready, there's a lot to do.

Your Sundays we should call them,
As I will wait hand, foot and finger on you,
Your Sundays we should call them,
Pick your wish, it might come true.

Sunday for Richard means,
Dinner promptly at two,
Sunday for Richard means,
An afternoon snooze.

Sundays are big days for me,
Cooking lunch, looking after Anthony,
Sunday's are big days for me,
Supplying love, joy and happiness for all three.

Our son enjoys Sundays too,
Spending quality time, entertaining you,
Our son enjoys Sundays too,
A lazy evening on the sofa, without a move.

Sundays are for Special Treats,
Sundays are for Roast Meat,
Sundays are for Family Fun,
Sundays are for Celebrating Life's Run.

I'm glad it's Sunday tomorrow,
Our favourite day of the week,
I'm glad it's Sunday tomorrow,
For, Together we shall be.

Joanna Dicks

Land Invasions

First came telephone poles, woody and brown
In every street in every town.
Then came pylons, electric, metallic
Bisecting the fields, visible to all traffic.
We have aerials reaching up to the sky
On every rooftop, conspicuous to the eye.
Next came satellite dishes with their magic ball,
Clinging like limpets against the wall.
Now there's phone masts going up, no permission
And accused of giving off dangerous emissions.
People protest and sometimes succeed
In blocking a mast if they feel there's a need
To protect the community from these unsightly apparitions,
That are another example of land invasions.

R Ramshaw

Prayer With Passion

you could be in a ward
in coma or chaos
confusion or pain or panic,
with only the power of refusal
to figures dimly discerned;
so many identities and murmurs
of voices, of strange isolation
or fearsome intrusion,
from which 'Lord have mercy'
and 'God preserve me,'
seem suitable prayers.

Monica Redhead

Night

Sun has long since finished burning,
Light expelled by dark returning,
Through the jewels of Heaven's crown,
The hand of night is reaching down.
Its fingers stretch across the sky,
Creep softly down to where you lie,
A bed of grass on open ground,
Where night throws shadow all around.
Its blanket steals the earth away,
And peaceful seems the end of day,
Night has no words or thoughts to bring,
Yet in your ears it seems to sing.
Like a soft and sacred blessing,
Feel the hand of night caressing.

But peaceful feelings in your heart,
Will very soon be torn apart,
The wind sounds like a ghostly whine,
Sends shivers up and down your spine.
As childhood fears come racing back,
Your courage starts to strain and crack,
That soothing hand upon your brow,
Seems somehow not so friendly now,
Those fingers that did gently stroke,
Around your neck begin to choke.
You thought the night would bring sweet dreams,
But now your mind for daylight screams.
Like Hell's unholy demon crew,
The hand of night is touching you.

Robert Solloway

Silver Shilling

It was only a silver shilling and I was nine years old
But oh! That silver shilling was worth its weight in gold
I took it to the cinema, to see the silver screen
And I tell you what I saw there was every child's dream
The darkness filled with colour and music filled my ears
I sat there so excited, my eyes they filled with tears
The fairy tale adventures, such giants I had never seen
Open mouthed in wonder as I licked on my ice-cream
It was only a silver shilling and now I'm growing old
But the memories that it gave me are worth their weight in gold

Sandra Wellbeloved

Gentleman Dick

'Tis wild weather said Jack to his sire,
Yes, gentleman Dick, we must be on time to fire,
If you're to catch your morning ride,
It'll be a long journey to a London borough.

But first I must quench this thirst with a long keg of ale,
O honourable Bess I do desire,
For we mustn't dilly dally at this dangerous hour,
Below this scarlet English sky we tread wild flower.

The long dash ride upon the howling wind,
We must leave this Yorkshire mire.
Now to apprehend a King's courtly coach my friend,
Stand and deliver gentlemen, it's my delightful jest I send.

It be a dire warning on this misty shire,
At the displeasure of His Majesty's realm;
Now, I shall relieve him of all he owns,
Of his chest of silver and his shiny gold.

For I have already torn down his proclamation of old,
O Mr Turpin, it is but highway robbery so bold.
For we are discouraged on this desolate highway,
For we'll be obliged to see you at your merry dance.

For it'll be a merry hanging you see for thee,
O come now gentlemen, for it cannot be you see,
For I have already died the jig of a hangman's lee,
Now come my faithful Bess, we must leave this English road and flee.

'Tis wild weather said Jack to his sire,
Yes, gentleman Dick, we must be on time to fire,
If you're to catch your morning ride,
It'll be a long journey to a London borough.

James Stephen Cameron

Long Gone

There'll be no park bench for me,
    or white trousered green bowls tournaments;
There'll be no doting over grubby grandchildren,
    or school concerts and sports events;
There'll be no trying to outlive some neighbourhood friend,
    or processions of funerals that I'll have to attend;
I'll be long gone.

There'll be no indignation at the rate of inflation;
    and no cursing politicians for their stupidity;
There'll be no circling of distant relation,
    and picking over the bones of an ancient me;
There'll be no searching for insurance policies,
    or letters of probate, mixed with solaces;
I'll be long gone.

And in a short time, when I'm all but forgot,
    except perhaps by a few,
Don't visit my grave, even on anniversaries;
I'll not be there, for even you.

Keith Sidwell

Home!

She sits sedately in her shoebox
Side by side with many alike
Along the clean carpeted corridor.
Memories missing in unfamiliar furnishings.
She brought only the scrapbook in her mind.
The pink chenille bedspread is hers
Matching the dressing gown on the door,
Both 'moving-in' gifts from her son.

He bought the TV too ~ little used,
Depressing news, programmes crude and rude,
Alien to her eighty years of settled life
Now ending in these uncluttered confines.
Gone are the sing-songs of yesterday,
The family gatherings she co-hosted.

The walls feel so close, pale,
Like tissue in her box, surrounding her.
They told her she will not fall here,
No stairs, no two up, two down to dust.
The only cobwebs now in her dulling mind,
No need to reach for them.
They'll festoon her thoughts until
They cocoon her scrapbook.

She hears to-ing and fro-ing in the passage,
A hoover buzzing along, soon to shatter her peace.
A chatty, slip-of-a-girl will come to 'put her straight'.
Then lunch ~ 'Wish they'd put bicarb in the greens,
Cabbage should be crisp and green not white and watery!'
Each day she feels more like a shoe in her box.
Well-weathered, well-worn, but comfy,
With still a few earthly miles left in her soul!

Pat Heppel

The Mirror

You were looking at me,
Half looking at you too,
And you said slowly and surely
'I will know all of you.'

I saw you looking at me,
Half looking at you too,
And I said to myself in no way
Will that ever be true.

But mirrors don't lie do they?
And I'm here looking at you
The mirror got smashed on the way
And I know all of you too.

Michele Busk

My First Day At Secondary School

I remember a day many years ago
How great it was
It really was significant
Out with the old and in with the new
There were many thoughts I had
Things I had never felt before

The school seemed so big to me
I wondered how I would fit in
So many people it was surprising
Feelings of fear and excitement entertained me
For a whole new world was opening up

Would this place swallow me?
How should I be?
Entering into another stage of life
Slowly growing into adulthood
Wonder and intrigue absorbed me
Into this place I would become immersed

Stuart Thomas

Heaven

Sunbeams drifting slowly by
A starlit, sunlit, moonlit, sky
Mountains tinted white with snow
Grasshoppers jumping to and fro
Marigolds and daffodils
Grow hand in hand on sunkissed hills
Bluebirds calling to their mates
Over silver streams and shining lakes
Ladybirds and butterflies
With boys and girls down rainbows slide
Goldfish swim in pools of blue
With water nymphs and mermaids too
Silver fountains, golden falls
Lollipops and aniseed balls
Wonder in its utmost phase
Such a place to spend our days
A land where danger no one knows
A land where beauty and fantasy flows
A land where no one rises at seven
Could this be that place we all call Heaven?

Oliver Ashby

Christmas Time

Christmas day, a favourite time,
A time of good cheer, and food most fine.
With ringing bells, and carol tunes,
And fir trees glittering in sitting rooms.

Decorations strung from wall to wall,
Merry Christmas to you is the friendly call.
Young children's faces beaming bright,
Because Father Christmas has got it right.

On Christmas morn, these children seen
Out on new bikes all shiny and clean.
All manner of toys are on display,
On this, the children's day of days.

Oven brown turkeys cooked to a turn,
With mince pies, and pudding, we all do yearn.
Christmas dinner it is, in many a home,
That brings home again, those that have roamed.

Grown ups at Yuletide have every reason,
To indulge in toasting the festive season.
Cold frost and snow will not deny,
A Christmas drink with friends nearby.

Just once a year, this day comes round,
When good wishes and happiness do abound.
So make the most of Christmas day
By celebrating the day, the traditional way.

B Acton

Barbara

Come with me my fair one
Across the great divide
Let's share our life together
Our thoughts as one, side by side

Your smile greets me with joy
Like dawn, heralding the bright face of day
Your deep lustrous brown eyes sparkle
Embracing me under your cloak of love
My whole being aflame with desire

My love for you is absolute
My heart, my soul, yours alone.

Joseph Worthington

Autumn Love

Autumn love is comforting ~
It's like an open fire
That glows behind each living coal
And fills you with desire.

Autumn love is mystery ~
A great big shining star
That looks down on 'the past' that's been
And made us what we are.

Autumn love is order ~
Preparing for next season.
Taking stock of what to do
And having a good reason.

The ground was soft with fallen leaves
Where once the snowdrops grew ~
When young hearts met with eyes aglow ~
Each moment fresh and new.

The ground was soft with fallen leaves
Where once bright flowers bloomed ~
When lovers' hearts beat as one
And minds were finely tuned.

The ground was soft with fallen leaves ~
It seemed that all had perished ~
But still hearts met and loved as one ~
For love is always cherished.

Pat Melbourn

I've Been Here Before!

Swimming is fun so they say
So that was my objective for today
Out of the drawer my costume came
Somehow it doesn't fit the same
Some places it seems to fit just right
But across the bum a little bit tight
Tight across the boobies too
A little more bosom comes into view
I think I have to realise
My body *again* has increased in size
Onward ~ to the diet book
To get that well-loved slimline look

Christine Robinson

Missing You

My world of roses round the door has gone forever
for my life changed the day you went away
You always said I'd miss you and now I know that's true
What do I miss? I miss you.

I miss the man I depended on, the man I loved so much
Who shared all those special years and thrilled me with his touch
My eyes have lost their sparkle, the spring has left my step
The joy of going home each day was lost with your last breath.
What do I miss? I miss you

On Sunday night I miss you most, at the dance before the new
week began
Monday morning I miss your kiss together with the early cup of tea
On Tuesday night a glass of wine with a video meant for two
Wednesday could have been gardening followed by a bath
Thursday night a cuddle or two with our Lucy in between
What do I miss? I miss you.

On Friday after work was done a meal down the pub, to save myself
a job
Then back to Saturday and crib for you and shops for me
Relax the weekend was here.
What do I miss? I miss you.

The days mentioned may have been rearranged, but depict my life
with you by my side.
It wasn't always harmony, for we had our differences
But you always looked after me and I hope I looked after you
I loved you every second and I know you loved me loads
What do I miss? I miss you.

My life has lost its meaning, my heart has lost its glow
But part of you will always be part of me.
What do I miss? Saying *'I love you'* to you.

Your lonely wife.

Valerie Ann Bellingham

Crooked Pictures

I seek solace
Silently search ~
Shallow, shapeless survival
Soulless, sightless seeing.
Sanctum of sorrow.

Tongues tongue tales,
Wag woes
Tut taut taunts;
Don't you know ~
Crooked pictures hang.

Weak, wasted words.
Soft, small someone
Snuggling so! So ~
Tell me again ~
Crooked pictures hang.

Ellen McEwan

Pen

Poised
Allowing the author
Time to think
Ready to skate
Like a girl in the rink

Enriching
A lined landscape of empty space
With its choreographed swirls
And liquid grace

Neutralising
The ambitious antics of powerful men
It's mightier than the sword
It's the humble pen

Gary Ball

Random Music

Upon a hill so softly layered in rich velvet green
Each blade shivers in unison with the breeze
As we lay hand in hand, not a word we need say
Filled with random music since nature here is free to play

Lying, listening to all the sounds, verdant world around
The fragrant peace around us deeply breathed
Sweet interruptions of the melody, flying percussion calls
With the wind, the music's tempo, how it rises falls

Oasis from daily grey, its noise, colours, daily roar
Tranquil peace for a while, drifting away heart and soul
If this is my moment, life ended, happy here to die
Such a beautiful place, amongst the music here to lie

A C Dancer

A Prayer Of Hope

O Lord for the animals we now pray,
For all those animals that we slay;
The cattle, pigs and flocks of sheep
That we are now putting to sleep.

O Lord for the farmers we now pray.
Help them through these troubled days,
As life for them has not been kind,
Give them hope and peace of mind.

O Lord for business we now pray,
For those who face ruin day by day.
It's for them this is a crisis time
As tourism and trade are in decline.

O Lord for the workers we now pray,
Those unemployed who have no pay;
The stress of this they have to bear.
Give them faith that they don't despair.

O Lord for the Government we now pray.
Help them to lead us, show them the way.
They really try and do their best;
This crisis has put them to the test.

O Lord for troubled times we now pray
That this epidemic will go away,
Freeing our animals from its pain,
Never to return to plague us again.

Francis Allen

Fen Country

Island country
Where villages stood
Moats and embankments
Protecting from flood.

Sheep grazed well
Around monasteries rich
Orchards, vines.
So long as the ditch, was there.
Churches still from times gone by.

Vermuyden thought to drain the fen
Aided by nobles and richer men
Who wanted to reclaim land
To use, stewards managing Nature.

They let more water out
Through canals, where flood
Ran swiftly onward to sea
And meandering rivers
Fine to view, did not
Have to carry the total burden.

And today the peat is nearly gone
Drained and dried and blown for a song, away in the air
So clay is left.

The land has sunk
The rivers are high
What to do, now? ~
We hear man cry

And the rivers and canals
Flow on
But beneath the waters,
Remains of wood
Where terra firma once proudly stood
Before the waters came
And the drovers' roads ran.

Hazel Smith

First Flight

We lived in Helensburgh by the Clyde
And it has happy memories for me.
On bicycles we travelled far and wide
Between Glen Fruin, Loch Lomond and the sea.
The uncle of two school friends lived in Rhu
And kept a sea plane on the Gareloch shore
And there one day in nineteen thirty-two
We did what we had never done before.
We knew that Uncle Tom was flying that day
So cycled up and met him on the beach.
The plane was moored not very far away
Requiring just an easy row to reach.
There were two cockpits in the little plane
So each in turn climbed in to take a ride
And what a thrill it was when my turn came
And we soared up above the Firth of Clyde.
I have been airborne many times since then,
But that first flight remains a memory
Of one exciting day when I was ten
And life stretched out towards Eternity.

Ian Purvis

Night Walk

Up to my ears I tug my coat collar,
Turtle my neck in and tuck down my chin,
A dog's plea I hear, he begs let me in.
My hands in soft wool gloves nestle encased
Cats run seek the hearth of a warm fireplace.
I walk past gold windows with draped filled lace.
Feet hurry, soles crunch on rigid water
As pools and puddles splinter then shatter
While a polished moon in a blushing sky
Shines down on lurex dusted rooftop tiles.
Diamond flecked cars dazzle both my eyes
Suspended ghosts of speech float in the air
My thick coat grows thin, I almost despair,
The door opens, amber warmth tints my hair.

Ethel Oates

The Waiting Game

I can't sleep,
I can't eat.
I'm restless every time,
Tossing and turning.
This is driving me crazy.

The telephone doesn't ring any more,
Mr Postman doesn't knock on my door.
This waiting seems to get me down,
It feels painful, I want to scream and shout.

I'll carry on waiting for you,
I'm sure you'll turn up soon.

Chandra

My First Boyfriend

I was just eleven and I liked to ride my bike.
An only child, to me it was pure delight.
Lucky me to live in a road by the sea.
In a newly built estate where building sites were great,
For exploration with a mate.
He had a bike and we had races ~
Great excitement in our faces.
Then one day he called for me.
'How would you like to come to tea?'
Might,' I said noncommittally.
I really didn't know what to say.
I'd really much rather go out to play.
'Come at four, Mum says it's OK.'
I told my Mother. She said, 'Why not?
He's only up the road.'
I frowned. 'He's spoilt it now ~ I just won't go.'
'You silly goose, why ever not?'
'I don't really like, him, not a lot.'
So I stood at my gate and thought a lot.
And he stood at his gate and waved a lot.
Then I went inside and shut the door.
Boys! I like my bike a whole lot more!

Peggy M J Smith

Granny Gregory's Alphabet
(With acknowledgements to The Children's Encyclopaedia)

A is for Abigail who Abseiled at Ayr;
B is for Benjamin Brought by a Bear;
C is for Catherine who Came with her Chum;
D is for David who Danced on his Drum;
E is for Edmund who Enjoyed it out East;
F for Francesca who Flambéd a Feast;
G is for Granny. Gone down the Glen;
H is for Henry who Hustled the Hen;
    H is for Hen and, I think you'll agree,
    It is also for Hannah who carried a banner
    And danced in the manner of chimps having tea.*
I for Irene who Intends to use Ink;
J is for Joseph who Jumped a high Jink
    And J is for Jonathan, also for James,
    J is the start of a number of names.
K is for Kate who Kept a large Kite;
L is for Lawrence who Laughed at the Light;
M for Michaela who Marched to the Mine;
N is for Norman, of Newts he caught Nine;
O is for Oswald who an Owl did Observe;
P is for Pia with a Pot of Preserve;
Q is for Quentin who Questioned a Quail;
R is for Robert who Rests on a Rail;
    R is for Robert and also for Rose
    Who Rambled to Ramsgate as everyone knows;
S is for Stephen whose Steed lost A Shoe;
T is for Thomas who Tried a Tattoo
    (not a picture on skin but a roll on a drum
    which tells people to look or listen or come);
U is for Ursula who Upset an Urn;
V is for Vivien with Volumes by Verne;
W for William who Went to the Well;

X is for Xavier who eXpects to eXcel;
Here's Y and Z who declare it a shame
To stay at the bottom without any name.

**Of course, she could dance perfectly well. She was just having fun.*

Catherine Gregory

What We Say About Our Environment

Whatever your view there's a little philosophy
A common bond of sense that makes everyone happy
Because living in a house is a lot of responsibility
And without one we're forever more reliant on society.

If you take it that modern man also seeks a living
He can't spend too much time on improving the general cause
But collectively he can make sense without too much thinking
And little less ghost of a town is left for the doubters.

I guess man moves around from time to time
And then it'll depend on whether sea or country inhabits
But with family on transport he can see a bit of both climes
And see if a green land or blue ocean predominates.

My present world is a bit of the artificial undefended by pressure group
Because human vanity by seaside promenade is a matter of task
Whilst the beauty of landscape is mirrored by erstwhile luminaries
I wish my town's brashness could be a little moderated.

I like natural variety such as in the Lakes
A lowland walk through trees followed by a mountain stamp of Gables
Enough to invigorate man and charge up his own self
A rich living experience of equal worthiness.

But I'm lucky I have a home and a quiet town to live in
Because fresh air and seaside aside it's enough for things written
And memories provide inspiration and dreams to explore
Whilst uncertainty is not what sustains my small thoughts.

David Lloyd

Song For Ardnamurchan

When I first set foot on that strange volcanic land
Of broken moors unfinished by God's hand
And I saw the vast and lonely sky
And I heard the curlew's desperate cry
Then the jilted beauty pierced me like a dart
I could neither stay nor could I take my heart

If Ardnamurchan can do this to me
Will I ever be free
To love again?
The winds of change invading from the sea
Have blown your sons and daughters far away
Why should they call me?

Too far away to meet with history
Who would record your cruel adversity?
One noble hero shipwrecked on your shore
Fled through your hills to fight in Charlie's war
No chronicle from some ancient writer's quill
You closed your doors and the hidden land lay still

Now Ardnamurchan's far away from me
But if ever I'm free
I will return
The sands of time in Sanna's distant bay
I'll feel beneath my feet and the winds will whisper
'Stay'

Albany McGregor

This Olde House

This olde house was once a home where we lived
that is my family and I all those years ago
Now somebody else lives in this place
the very thought causes a tear to fall from my face.

In this place I lived with my family
that is with my Father, Mother and two Brothers
And indeed each of us cherished the moments
shared all of those years ago.

I think back now to all of the happy times
the Birthdays, Easters and Christmas's spent here
for all of the tempers that did flare
and for all the times we cared when one of us was ill
every moment that was sad even those that were glad
they all were important every single moment
now those memories are where they should be, buried in the past.

Peter J Grayson

Duration

Give in to a heart of mellow time,
Unfolding images of long ago.
Loves forsaken, trudging home to truths unshaken,
Roses climb round every door.
The mill grinds out its honest flower.
Waters gush, paddles strike the floor
Of streams and rivers, aplomb, with fish galore.
There's pike and bream. Perch and roach
Salmon too ~ 'Oh what a dream',
Of haywain harvests, cherubs bare,
Clothes didn't mater, let others stare.
Apples gleam, and pears that ripen,
Low boughs are laden, with May rose white.
Buttercups lift ~ a token, yellow bright,
And kiss the dewdrops. A glistening sight
Telling tales of homes, grim and cold
Beds of straw, hymns of slaves
Of masters grim, stern and bold,
Still desires remain, though bent the knee.
Quicken, soon, to early graves.
Their smiles of love, families told.
How soon they leave this blessed fold.
To beg and scrape, on fields green, so cold.
But never murmur, for forest gate.
Where pines aspire, as heavens wait
So their duration was somewhat spare
Even so, they gave life, a scare.
With love and fellowship, lifting time
As though tribulation, improves the wine.
Still clasping hands of love, devotion rhyme.

A Boddison

We Never Seem To See

7am and I wake up in a sweat
waiting for the girl of my dreams
to be with me for all eternity,
I need her so badly that I can't go on
when will she be mine,
can you tell me what I have to do
to make her mine,
we may talk but
we never seem to see
each other the way we want to,
the night time comes and
she's still not mine.

Chris Barber

Untitled

I have wanted to know your name since forever. Alas!
Knowing your name has not brought me closer to you.
Mistily I move towards, away from,
Towards, away from
The unchanging Truth.

I place my own hands inside my own head
And twist my mind round
To face myself.
In the Truth I would be.
But I still have not enough of that
Which makes us make the jump.

I reassured myself that with time, I would
Small step by small step, no! What I know as
Safe step by safe step, get there.

But it seems that reality is not made of that,
For if we move about in that which
We claim to know,
We wonder aimlessly in the safety of this world
And are
Thus continuously lost.

Change in our own safe illusionary world
That we create, is no change at all.

Only when we are disturbed enough
Are we forced to make a true change,
Like it
Or not.

Basia Palka

Arachnophobia

The dead eyes of darkness stare you down,
Stock-still and silent your blood runs cold
But more than that ~
Vein slashing, brain cracking, rose shattering, liquid nitrogen cold.
Your bones turn to milk.
Your rationality extends eight hairy legs and scuttles away.
The fear is all encompassing, a straight jacket inhibiting your
every move.
The colour drains from your soul leaving blackness.
Just black.
Just deep black.
Black as deep as the dead eyes of darkness that stare you down.

Peter Miles

Our Neighbours

I see again those streets and houses
Near where I lived and played
So familiar in my memory
As they were and still today
I remember well this other house
But not those two sitting there
An elderly couple so happy
Sitting down without a care
But soon they rise and go indoors
I want to call our clear
Stop! This is not your house you know
My friend's family lived here
We played together in this garden
And in the mountains we would play
I'd wait for him to go to school
The family's gone now, sad to say
So no-one really owns these buildings
For we are just passing through
This life like simple travellers
On the journey, we all make too.

Terry Daley

Chew Valley Lake

Walking around the lake at Chew Valley,
Negotiating the mud and puddles left over from Winter,
The evening sun setting on the horizon
Shimmering in the cold, grey water.
Ducks, their beady eyes bright and alert with mischief
Paddle along contentedly, avoiding the reeds along the bank.

Reeds. Thick, straw-coloured, coming straight out of the water,
Not very pretty, they don't sprout flowers or berries, or even leaves.
Utility plants, useful for paper-making or as mouthpieces on
woodwind instruments.
That's where their beauty lies, in literature and music ~
Nothing much to look at, yet indispensable in transmitting beauty
Around the world to anybody who's interested.

A rustle in the reeds and a closer look reveal
A grebe nestling amongst the plants.
A really close look is necessary, the reeds are so thick,
They hide the grebe, protecting it from danger.
A lifeline for birds, no doubt for mammals too;
Reeds, the plant that hid a basket, a lifeline for a baby in danger,
Freedom for a nation too long in bondage.

A tiny nation, lodged in the middle of great powers,
A tin-pot nation, not worth much by worldly standards,
Yet chosen above the others for a great destiny;
Saved by a baby hidden in the reeds,
Presided over by a youngest son interested in poetry and sheep;
Then a baby again, born in a stable to working-class parents,
Who grew up to die an undignified criminal's death.

A death that spelt life.
Like the insignificant reeds that saved
An insignificant nation;
So an insignificant death saved
Thousands of people, insignificant
And otherwise from a fate worse
Than death itself.

Kathy Rawstron

Embarrassment

We all have embarrassing moments, when we would like to go ~
Hide into a corner, that no one us might know.
I'd like to share such a moment, that happened to me one day.
When I wanted to vanish, out of everyone's way.
Was going to lead a meeting, running a little bit late.
Rushed got myself ready, at quite an incredible rate.
Sitting in the front at the table, glanced down at my shoe.
Looked down again in horror, it really couldn't be true.
On my right foot a brown shoe.
On my left, would you believe a blue.
Tried to tuck my feet under the table, that no one else would see.
Knew if someone noticed, how amused they would be.
Nothing I could now do about it.
Try to act naturally, as there I did sit.
When the meeting was over, tried to brave it out, and say
Made such a silly mistake, because of a busy day.
Must admit made me more careful, in what I now do.
Don't want a repeat performance, with one brown, and one
blue shoe.

E Griffin

Memories

The last few months of my Earthly existence
Hold unhappy memories for you 'My Dear'.
The sight of my poor battered body, lingers yet.
Causing you distress for my suffering, and maybe
Guilt that you were not there to save me.
Anger at others who could have/should have done more.

Stop, let go of it all, right now 'Sweetheart'
It was only the overcoat I was wearing at the time,
That was damaged. My Soul was still perfect.
Just as yours is. Nobody and nothing can damage
Or hurt the Soul within. Bricks and mortar
with the help of builders, can make a house.
It is the people who live inside, that make it a Home.

Remember 'Happy Times' my Daughter.
Let the memories touch your Heart with Love.
Then let the feeling continue up to your beautiful face
Bringing a smile. By the time it reaches your eyes
The Sun will be shining once more within your Soul.
The reflection of your light will reach me in a twinkling of an eye.
Every time you appreciate beauty in any way shape or form.
You will be seeing me as clearly as the nose on your face.

Dolly Little

Reading

Come read to me your poems, as you sit before me now
For I have dwelt among the dead, and smelt the breath on
Satan's brow

Fling your flame into the spume of fire let it drift
That green dank wire, let it worm and spiral clear
wave and torrent, clean and sheer

Pressing, crashing jutting lashing calming shadow towing flapping
Like a dream of discontent, a wretched beast sentient
To stand upon that peak of joy and know the moment
Advancing on the shadows deep

A crouching peasant's gaudy cloth,
A slothful present in a tawdry trough
Night-times Dandy; grounded on a sudden rock
flinging far and free
And Saturn's glowing embers an appointment on the lee
And I will read your poems in the dark and secretly.

Pluto

The Family Of The Church

We thank you for your church Lord
And folk of kindred thought,
For help we give each other,
For friendship and support.

We thank you God for Jesus,
Our everlasting friend,
Who leads, inspires and blesses,
Whose mercy knows no end.

Now let us serve the Master
And be one family,
And may His love shine through us
That everyone may see ~

He is the world's redeemer,
God's, gracious, Holy Son,
Who, through His death on Calvary
Salvation for us won.

And so dear Lord and Saviour
Be in our hearts today,
And guide us on life's journey
We humbly ask and pray.

Lord, give your benediction
While in your house we meet,
And help us join our voices
And praise to you repeat.

Amen to God the Father,
Amen to God the Son,
Amen to Holy Spirit,
The Godhead ~ three in one.

Edgar Hucker

His Pain

I look at him
So strong and tall
Walking with sticks
Thanks to a fall

He cried so hard
That terrible day
When an accident
Took all he knew away

We struggled each
And every week
To make a few
Lousy ends meet

He will never be
The same again
Now he has pain
That'll never end

But I'll be here
To help him through
Without him here
My life is through

Mary George

For My Daughter

We may not always see eye to eye,
And sometimes we make each other sad.
But every time you smile at me,
I forget the reason I am mad.

When I may not like the things you do,
And I don't agree with what you say,
The moment you tell me 'I love you,'
All the bad times simply go away.

There are days we make ourselves so cross,
And it seems we don't like each other.
But I'll always love you very much,
You're my daughter and I'm your mother.

Kaz

Adventure On A Station Platform

Steam breath exhaled
Mingled autumn chill,
giving tell to lover's conversation
overheard,
on station platform.

He said . . .
'If I touch your hand on greeting
or kiss your cheek on leaving . . .
would our friendship sullied be?
Do you want to
stay a friend . . . or
when I look at you
should I my lover see?
To decide is not for you nor me . . . but we . . .'

She said . . .
'Ours is an adventure
for which there is no measure,
lest you can calibrate emotion.
Let us wait,
and . . . if agreed we . . .'

But then
a train clanked in
all smoke and smuts.
A thrill of breath commotion

meant . . .
I never heard the answer . . .
to this adventure on a station platform.

D I Ross

Jigsaw

He was a mischievous Skewbald
Grabbing washing from my line
But he was mine,
My first and only pony.

When my day's work was done
Teaching him manners was fun.
His purpose in life, to escape being caught.

Once in the stable
The harness I'd bought
To fit it I was able
And off we would go for a ride,
Jigsaw, my first and only pony.

Irene Beeson

My Dream

I dream of a home of my own,
Deep in the countryside, home alone.
A greyhound rescue centre, it's what I'd love.
To keep all these wonderful dogs safe.
To walk them in the woods.
To watch them play with each other.
They would always be my babies.
To them, I'd be their mother.
It'd give them a warm bed and food,
Safe shelter from the night,
And when they feel any fear,
I'd hold them in my arms, nice and tight.
I love greyhounds, I've always had,
They are so full of good, never bad.
One day, I hope my dream will come true,
And 'Racer's Paradise' will come to light.
How my dull world, would be so very bright.

Diane Campbell

Salty Tears

to the paper they fall
to the ink they smudge
to the words they merge
to the meanings they soak
against the paper more do drop
reading onwards they don't stop
to every word one will fall
to every letter another one follows
to every line to every dot
they continue to drop down to the page
reading on they still descend
faster and harder
with every one an emotion falls upon the words
with every drop a question is contained
to every thought one will plunge
into the depths of the writing
memories pour
feelings flow
these salty tears don't go
these salty tears never slow.

Katy Morley

Clouds

Tonight the sky was pink enveloped in chiffon,
I saw a red flight of swans,
But, when I looked again
The reds and pinks
Became a mass of purple flowers.
These colours were those of nature's,
So how could I argue.
To paint was my wish
I knew that it would not last
For, as the day was coming to an end
These colours would soon diminish
Never to return again.
But, tomorrow the swans will be horses
And the flames perhaps ships,
Again, a sight to remain
But only for a second in time.

Caroline Frances Ballard

Paradise Fields
(Dedicated to all at 'Eastridge Farm')

Supreme, salmon-pink creatures
Happily nudging the soil in search of a morsel.
I see them and I love them,
In the field, I see their fun.
Their beauty will remain eternal.

I saw what you did
And millions of teardrops could not stop
The pain . . .
A human-being without a conscience
You will never be forgiven

And I pray that these star-studded animals
Are in paradise fields of hay
Safe,
Because all of us think it's such a waste
And now when I drive past, I see
Your special homes tossed aside
And all around the thick smoke
Burning all our hope
All this future has brought is empty fields
Now full of earth
And my favourite pigs murdered
In the fields where they played.

L J Allison

Clear Life

We have children that cannot breathe
For the air is not clear
For car fuel drives along our street.

For sprays we use, for smells of sweetness.
For the dirt on the street, that we have made.
For ozone layer we made.
Life should change for better not worse.

Use a scoop, when you take your dog.
Others will tread and spread.
Just take one through to bed with you.
Clear life for ozone layer.

Patricia Maloney

Love

Love is putting
the other persons happiness before yours
even if
that means letting them go
love is not selfish
love is not about you
or who you love
it's about
the love, in the heart of the person

You know you love someone
when you can smile
when you let them go

Love is not sad
love is beautiful
you have to feel it in your guts
in your heart
it's hard to explain
love
is simply a smile
not a tear

Tracey Rose

A Christmas Scene

There's a stable, there's a star,
There's a holy feeling,
There are wise men from afar
At the manger kneeling.

Listen to the song on high,
'Gloria'.
Let God's love light up your sky.
Follow the star!

There are shepherds from the hillside,
Eyes with angel-fire glowing,
There's a donkey, gently resting
And the cattle lowing.

Listen to the song on high,
'Gloria'.
Let God's love light up your sky.
Follow the star!

There's a special family
With a baby bringing
Peace on earth from heaven above.
Hear glad tidings ringing!

Listen to the song on high,
'Gloria'.
Let God's love light up your sky.
Follow the star!

Gloria Joice

A New Love

How do you tell
Your old love
You have found a new love?

What do you say to someone
You have been with for so long?
How can you tell them?
What can you say?
You don't love them
After so many years.

They would not understand
How your new love
Makes your heart jump,
Your body go hot and cold,
Her lips so warm and loving,
Her ways so warm and kind.

Eddie Sheldon

Hog The Mike

(For Nicky of the Masons pub, Old Swan, for being a muse)

'Oh no'
Went the mumbles and the sighs.
Here is again
Old 'Hog the mike' . . .
Psyche him, psyche him
As they might.
He'd still get up
To do yet another number.
Being so single minded
And just as doubles tight.
The karaoke DJ says to him
'Others want to sing again.'
But his words to him are in vain.
The cells of reason
Being dead in his brain.
For now he's on drunken auto-pilot . . .
While the audience?
Just think he's on an ego trip and vain.
But they don't know his story
How could they!
In fact . . . why should they?
The words slurred as they may . . .
For him, have some deeper meaning to say.
They're a comfort, a reminder of his loss
A glimmer . . . in his world of dross.
You see . . .
She was everything, she was 'Boss'
So please remember
When he renders Elvis and co ~ to death
It's his life . . . it's his breath.

Malcolm Peter Mansfield

Dogs ~ God's Creations Too!

Dogs ~ black ones, white ones!
Dogs ~ thin ones, tubby ones!
    Brown, gold, grey, multi-coloured!
Dogs ~ souls in their eyes, hearts as well!

Oh, how they trust us,
    need us, want us.
We must respond ~
    no cruelty with beating, starving.
'Yes' to play-times, fun-times, 'walkies'!
'Yes' to responding to dogs whose souls
    are in their eyes, hearts as well!

Rosalind Weaver

The Hospital Porter

Dilwyn was a porter
With trolley, clean and bright
He wheeled the live ones in by day
And the dead ones out at night.

He did his job with diligence
Though the pay weren't up to much
So he put some jam upon his bread
By moonlighting, and such.

Then came a day, a fateful day
It was his finest hour
They made him a manager
And gave him lots of power.

For equal opportunities had struck
And management had run amok
Instead of pushing bod's about
He's in admin, with lots of clout.

Gone were the porter's coat and boots
To be replaced by Burton suits
Platform shoes, to make him tall
And tie, that really said it all.

A single hurdle now remained
To manage ~ Dilwyn must be trained
A seminar would do the trick
To show our hero wasn't thick.

With filofax and mobile phone
Dilwyn really felt at home
Anticipating being top of class
Dilwyn's eyes shone, just like glass.

His training session was quite brief
His tutors stared in disbelief
Despite promotion overnight
Dilwyn could neither read nor write!

John Hill

Dragon Slayer

(For my annoying little brother)

A flickering tongue
A curving grin
A gleaming eye
A pointed chin

A glinting sword
A worried face
A poised shield
An armour case

Flame meets metal
Metal meets flame
The soldier steps forward
The Princess to claim

It raises its head
And roars to the moon
Its wings are outstretched
But it rises too soon

The knight jumps behind him
And plunges his knife
Deep into its hide
Which takes the beast's life

The dragon's hushed breathing
Builds one final wail
And it utters defeat
With a flick of its tail

The hero strides over
To embrace his new Queen
The fairytale ends here
To start a new scene

Sarah Bridges (13)

Angel

Angelis, my dark angel,
Comes to me in tortured dreams.
Touches my trembling flesh,
Burns my soul with darkest eyes,
Enslaves me with desire
Mere words could not describe.
Warm flesh on cold flesh,
Fire and ice,
Bodies and souls entwined.

Angelis, my dark hero,
His soul both cursed and blessed.
Protector of the innocent,
Defender, dark avenger,
Tortured by a passion
No mortal man could bear.
Mysterious and lonely,
Fighting evil souls,
On an eternal quest
He walks the darkest streets
A cruel destiny
He bears alone.

Jane Findlay

Little Eyes Of A Child

Little eyes of a child
you fill my heart with love
As I look into your eyes
I see your tears
of a pain you cannot word
too scared to speak aloud
silence, made you not to speak a word,
A tiny soul, too broken
Too damaged to mend
No one to speak out your pain,
they turn their backs and
hang their heads in shame
and never look back
to ease your pain
Break the silence of a
child's world

Kirsty Keane

Baa . . . Baa . . . White Sheep!

Little Bo-Peep, asks Baa, Baa, White Sheep, 'Have you any clue,
As to why on earth this foot-and-mouth scourge should
afflict you;
Why this calamity has made your species the scapegoat,
Forcing humans to resort to 'animal holocaust'?'
'Nay,' bleats Baa, Baa, White Sheep ~ 'We supplied humans wool
and meat,
We also gave them milk to make the most delicious cheese,
But now, savagely, they cull and kills us mercilessly,
In one combined operation ~ civil and military ~
Of 'Gulf-War' magnitude, and led by a Brigadier chap,
Following the 'foot-and-mouth-enemy', as on a Map,
Slaughtering, burning, rendering, burying at full stretch,
Taking 'pot-shots' at terrified ewes and lambs out of breath,
Chasing wounded sheep around a field as in a fox hunt,
Seeing panic in lambs' eyes ~ indomitable torment.'
Logistically twenty thousand slaughtered every day,
Briefed by Whitehall's Minister 'Agricola', ~ to cull and slay,
Adding to the mountain of dead livestock nearing million,
With burials halted due to bore-hole water pollution:
Incineration emits 'plague' in smoke, and is windswept,
So, trials on liming, with firebreak-policy, are firmly kept.
As this crisis will cost nine billion pounds to the country,
In Farmers' losses, and tourism, early in the century.
'Should Blair put off the Elections?' ~ ask the Media magnates ~
This slogan on a carcass Truck ~ Farmers' fury indicates!
Killings by man of sheep that gave Jason the golden fleece,
Recoils to square one: Shouldn't Whitehall start cloning *'Dollies'*?
One last quiz to the 'civil-military-combine' ~ white sheep asks,
Should humans contract a contagious disease, en masse,
Will these same Supremos exterminate the populace, rod, line
and sinker?
That's the sixty million dollar question, White Sheep, waits for
an answer!

Welch Jeyaraj Balasingam
May 2001

Ah!

Ah! How can I let you see
Can I let you feel this sense of me
If it starts with implicit accusations of betrayal
For not being the perfect ideal
There's this and there's that
There's roses and there's proses
Dressed of scent, of colours, of thorns
Undressed in words
Of which I do not know
If so I show myself or I hide
And so they are part of me

Ah! This trying to make sense
Of the senseless state of evolutional wholeness
Reaching for the ideal
Wanting it perfectly delivered into being
Yet, can we be open and still
Can we feel the vulnerability
The shadow of the soul in us
Tugging at the egotistical coat we wear so well
Can we feel our core
Without shrinking back to hide it
Can we be at peace with
And willing to take as our own
The very thing that compel us
Perpetual in its elusiveness
To the desired mint state

Ah! And we want a mirror
We want a mirror of light
Yet, can we be true to the desired reflection
Or are we a distortion going into space
Reverberating to reality
Holding us on and on
On the ties of:
Ah! How can I let you see!

Celia Maria Paulo

From First To Last

Summers come and winters go.
Nature, yearly takes her course.
Beginning with cold, frosty first of January.
A cycle of life, mind, body, spirit, a sanctuary.

Looking back to times past.
Thought of mind, needs no great task.
First open eyes, to grasp of hand.
Those first few steps, childlike feel of 'grand'.

A high pitch spoken word of anger
Go smack, not hard, cools paddy and dander.
Standing, sitting, all on one's own.
A big person now, see how I've grown.

First day arrives, now to school.
Will I be bright or someone's fool.
Skip, hop in sunshine or pouring rain.
'Best days of your life', is told ~ so gain.

Marriage one, for better or worse.
Always, not, divorce is prevalent, feelings a curse.
First born a treasure, to have and to hold.
Purse empty. Where! The pavements filled with gold.

Struggle with hurdles, sadness and pain.
In mind, calculating obstacles, tomorrow will remain.
Memories looking back with calm of choice.
Life lead with lessons in one's own voice.

Years have now taken their toll.
Many firsts have travelled this way.
Some to change, others to accept.
Make the most of firsts ~ all ~ without regret.

The chapter now closes, heaven sent ~ cannot stall.
Waiting, ready to take His first call.
Was life worth it, you may now ask.
Locked away the answer, tight in one's own cask.

Chrissie T

Relaxing In Phillip's Park

Taking the night air in the park
Sitting relaxing before it gets dark
Gazing up to a darkening sky
Pink clouds and grey float on by.

In the quiet beneath the trees
Not even the rustle of the leaves
Or another sound to be heard
Except the call of a solitary bird.

In the distance a single light
From a tower block nearly out of sight
Then whisperings, a laugh and a sigh
And still the clouds float on by.

So enjoying what is simple in life
Don't need the hustle and bustle and strife
This pleasant scene is enough for me
It offers peace and tranquillity.

Sheila Graham

Untitled

It was a normal day, the sky was grey
And everything was easy.
But in my mind, no normal grind,
I felt a peace within me.

Oh, so cool and Oh, so clear,
The purity, the beauty.

Now from that day, I change my way,
I live for now, I'm happy
The honesty and simple joy,
No fake, no fraud, real quality.

And now you see the real me,
So cool, so clear,
No mess, no stress,
Tranquillity.

Mickey Meloche

King Of The Road

King of the road ~ stately and autocratic
A diminutive five foot three he strode,
Continuously traversing streets and lanes
Of this county for many, oh many a year.

Spring and summer, autumn too, even in
Winter he would just woo the weather;
Aloof, self-confident, content ~ yet never
A room he'd rent, whatever the time of year.

Roughly hewn staff grasped firmly in hand ~
Not used to walk, but frequently to stand
And view a scene he'd scanned beyond the
Sights of me and you, throughout the years.

Pretty tidy, usually clean, belongings trussed
In a neat small sack jauntily slung across
His back, and tied by rope a billy-can swung,
In his proud and wandering years.

Knitted cap upon his head, occasionally he
Wore a spread of stubbly beard; he rarely
Spoke ~ but sometimes, with dignity, took a 'smoke'
From kindly hand, in passing down the years.

Never a frown upon his face, seemingly living
Within himself without one tiny space for
Other folk ~ maybe to him we're just a joke,
All these long and lonely years.

Now no longer can he stride, he must abide
City side; with majesty supreme he sits for throne
Upon a stone, safely surveying what passes by ~
Still seeing more than you or I ~ in his declining years.

I pray that God has kept a special place
For such as he who, unlike you and me, have need to step
Outside the daily race ~ and sacrifice themselves maybe
Just to live free, within their space of years.

Betty Jervis

Landscape

The joy, the overwhelming thrill,
Of standing high on a Herefordshire hill,
Observing the gently rolling land
Sculpted by the Master's hand.

Majestic trees of oak and beech
So very near, yet out of reach,
Provide a canopy for sheep
When resting on the hillside steep.

Rows of poplar here and there
Point their fingers to the air,
Just like soldiers in a row
Where daffodils and daisies grow.

Hedgerows thick with may and elder
Honeysuckle, growing wilder,
Hiding robin, blackbird, wren,
Cosy in their leafy den.

Of this sight I never tire
Sunsets spreading like a fire,
Don't let progress spoil this sight,
Surely we should have the right

The right and will for preservation
Let us try to keep our Nation
By uniting as a band,
Forever a green and pleasant land.

Ann Boyd

Here Stand I . . .

Great giant of gothic majesty,
silent witness to all time bears.
Facets of stone, eyes of glass,
I watch the tide of change.

Through plague and fire, war and strife
I stand so proud and tall.
Sadness and sorrow, victory and joy
is the endless dance of life.

Ravages of time, wind and rain
left me pitted, scarred and worn.
A lattice of pipes my outer dress
as I'm restored for this new dawn.

And as the sound of revellers
rings through my stony veins
I think of all the happy times
in my near millennial reign.

Like the many joyous times
that my aged bells did ring
calling Christians to celebrate
the birth of Christ the King.

You all say this millennium
is the only one you'll see,
but for me, time is irrelevant
and I am eternally free!

Thomas Bilbrough (12)

Ledbury Ghost Walk

We all felt a tingle of anticipation
at the thought of a ghostly walk,
clustered together under the old Market House
in hushed voices we did talk.

Our eerie guide appeared before us,
with flowing robes and grotesquely painted face,
telling us to follow behind her
she led the way walking at a very brisk pace.

The first haunted place we came to
was the New Inn of old
and the story of the ghostly male figure
made everyone's blood run cold.

The Seven Stars next with its beautiful floral attractions
hardly seemed the place for an unfriendly ghost,
but tales of possible lost chimney sweeps and priest holes
were told us by our spooky host.

On to the Barrett Browning Institute,
built as a tribute from a poet to his lover.
The building now houses Ledbury library
and hides many a story under its own cover!

The Feathers' quaint rear courtyard
with its hanging baskets and flowered bowers.
Here we were told of ghostly footsteps
that were heard in the night time hours.

The old Talbot with its panelled dining room
where cavaliers and roundheads fought,
then the reported sounds of long gone carriage wheels
to our attention was brought.

The lounge with its beautiful fireplace
on which mantle piece sits a silver coloured jar.
It is not a liquid spirit that causes its lid
to suddenly fly off and land further afar!

The Royal Oak in Ledbury Southend
more tales of ghostly happenings here.
We wondered why the ghostly late drinker
was not on spirits only a tankard of beer?

On to a Solicitor's establishment
where a poor girl met a grisly fate
and down old Cabbage Lane
even now, walking down there I hate.

A tomb of the Sexty family
invites a walk of twenty times round its stone.
Supposedly to raise a long gone spirit
who, if woken would probably wail and moan.

To Green Lane by Dog Hill wood
where the soldiers did ride down,
and the haunted Cut Throat Lane story
that made us all cringe and frown.

Lastly to the Horseshoe Inn
where cellar beer taps were turned off and on
and the white spirit seen in the bar
was not a drink but suddenly was gone.

A strange but enjoyable evening
and before it came to a close,
we found our own spirits in the Feathers
which brought a pleasant warm tingle to our toes!

Elizabeth Brace

She

Caring, loving, this was she,
Fragile and tender her anatomy,
Welded together by her kiss,
A sensation not to miss.

Soothing and comforting the feel of her hands,
Nature's way of showing she understands,
Stunning and elegant her long blonde hair,
Yet nothing compares to the clothes she wears.

Passionate and intimidating her crystal blue eyes,
Another part of her overwhelming disguise,
All reason why she belongs to me,
Why she'll always be my destiny.

Julian Old

To A Memory

Painted lady in sunlights glow
Each seasons change to love
Down winding lanes wild flowers grow
The primrose and foxglove.

Upon the moorlands purple hue
Heather sways in summer breeze
In the valley away from new
A village nestles by the trees.

With waters journey to sea begun
Rising springs so crystal clear
Its dance on mossy rock to run
Always changing with each year.

Granite soldiers standing tall
In record of ageless history
While sheep lay sheltered by the wall
Of magic, myth and mystery.

Descending mists that conceal
Hidden dangers beneath my feet
Oh pounding heart what do you feel
For the fears you now must meet.

Winters blanket of crisp, white snows
Covers all from tor to tor
But on Janes grave there lies a rose
A promise filled for ever more.

Harold R Bickham

The Wings Of Change

Mallards' Winter plumage
Of iridescent green,
Shimmering against the water,
As they swim and wash and preen.
The flashes on their wing tips
Vary with each one,
Look different at every angle,
Change colour in the sun.
The other ducks have also changed,
Much brighter than before
With coats of many colours,
Will last but three months more.
The process is beginning now
To find this season's mate,
Stretching necks and bobbing heads
Are all familiar traits.
But in the Winter sunshine
It's playtime all the way,
Except when kind folk bring some bread
To keep hunger pangs at bay.
They run as fast as their legs will go
In order to be first,
They eat non-stop and don't draw breath
Until they're fit to burst.
Whilst the scattered crumbs are taken
By seagulls, terns and crows,
The ducks and swans return to preen,
Their contentment clearly shows.
This ritual is repeated
Each time some bread is thrown,
Their appetites insatiable
But their behaviour quite well known.

When Springtime comes, all fit and strong
They hide their nests with care,
Lay and tend their clutch of eggs
And hatch their ducklings there.
From balls of fluff to downy feathers,
They grow so very fast,
Mature, develop, constantly change
Their plumage, each season's past.

Susan Small

The Gateway Of Noon

As light clings like precious fruit
To a bricked gateway where no mortal walks
In the heat and brightness of noon
As shadows lengthen and merge
Across time wearied stone
Before a carpet of yellowed grass and weed
Scattered stones and dead leaves
Embrace the shade of this solitary soul
While traffic both metal and flesh
Hurry by unseeing on the tide of the hour
Talking and laughing in a melancholy tone
As blossoms rejoice and fall
Like Christians to the lions
Of apathy and lethargy
To the realm of blind and deaf
Holding temporary sway
Over the gateway of noon

Paul Andrew Jones

A Winter's Sunday

I rise quite early, the wife's first cuppa,
Yes, after my ablutions I'll get another.
Then 'tis the wafting odour of toast,
And thoughts of the Sunday roast.
Oh! My tablet, I nearly forgot,
But not before the washing up.
Hats and coats on for the pm walk,
The inevitable chatter, the friendly talk.
We're nearly home, we think of a brew,
The tea I'll make for just us two.
We're inside now in our sheltered bliss,
Coats on pets, give TV a miss.
Get out the Scrabble that wholesome game,
Without which nothing appears the same.
'Tis six o'clock now, looking forward to tea,
And watch a modicum of TV.
Our eyes get sleepy, it's nearly eleven,
Soon to be tucked up in upstairs heaven.
Another Sunday over, another night's here,
Then 'tis Monday again so very clear.
A day so stark like a flag unfurled,
As outside we go to face the real world.

Nigel T Membury

A Lady In Waiting

She holds her breath as the sun moves down.
The roses he gave her are in full bloom, mirroring the colour of
her cheeks.
She gazes at the lions on the shield next to her unfinished sewing.

The scent from the roses surrounds her as she paces
back and forward across the square stones of the floor.
She holds her breath as the sun passes the top of the window.

Her fingers shake with the needle in her hand.
The cat curls up beside her as she tries to finish her lace rose.
She gazes at the shield, next to the white threads the cat has
unravelled.

Behind her a petal falls from a rose
landing between two harsh stones. It goes unnoticed.
She holds her breath as the sun moves behind the trees.

She hears a noise from beyond the oak door.
She knows her love is lost, they have come for her.
She gazes at the lions on the shield, next to a piercing metal tool.

Her face loses all its colour as the last petal falls from the rose.
Her hand passes across the finished lace as they break through
the door.
She holds her breath as the sunsets
gazing at the shield, her blood colours the petals and the lace rose.

Linda M Adams

Don't, Can't And Can

I *don't* possess wealth beyond measure
Or a box filled to the brim with treasure,
I *don't* have the skill to ease your pain
So you can live your life to the full again,
I *can't* turn daylight into night
Or make it rain when the sun's shining bright,
I *can't* make you say yes if you want to say no
Or make you go fast when you need to go slow,
But I *can* be beside you in thought every day
With a love that is deeper than words can convey.

Janice Smith

Candlelight

Candlelight I enjoy your quiet consoling illuminance.
It soothes my troubled thoughts
And lulls the tenseness of my mind
Dispelling the days' depressing clouds of doubt,
Blending my mood to the rhythmic silence of your velvet dance.
Reliant, steadfast, you have always been, shall be,
And like oil are man's ancient friend.
The genie of darkness before you retreats,
And softly melts away.

Inspiration of incandescent light, yet affinity you share
With lowly glow-worm or brightest star.
I Harmonise with your soft glow
As did the muse of long ago.
His thoughts inspired by the cup and your gentle light,
And thus did dream his sweet thoughts of romance and Love.
Your sure soft touch will always be there
To enhance a human ceremony.

Steady, sweet as at the altar of repose,
Or at the Romance of a table
Where vows of love will outlive the rose
May my troubled thoughts soar away,
Companion with the soot in the tip
Of thy fulfilled flame.
And may my spirit in Peace to be the same.

Thomas Wylie

Who Am I?

I am a human being,
Created by Almighty God!
In His own image and likeness
And truly blessed.

Who is God?
God is the creator of all things
Seen and unseen
I and all mankind are microcosms of God.
God is unconditional love.

Frank Findlay

Heidi's Lighthouse

Want to go for a walk?
We bundle into the car
You, me and grandma
And grandpa holds the door
It won't take long
Ten minutes and we're there
Along the coast to the leas
And Heidi's favourite place

Head alert
Eyes bright
Ear up . . . one always flops down
We tumble out of the car
The smell of the sea
And stripes of the lighthouse
The cry of the gulls
And we're off
Heidi pulling for freedom
Through cowslips and daisies

Heidi come!
Chase the Frisbee, catch the ball
From me, to you, to grandma
And grandpa holds the coats
'Look at that little dog,' children shout
Oh the joy, the trembling excitement
With Happy Birthday memories
Carried on the wind
A place for dogs and riding school horses
Look out for practising golfers

Heidi come!
Pulling through feathers and clover
Panting back to the car
Carefully with ice-creams to share
From me, to you, to grandma
And grandpa juggles with his
Licking our fingers
Licking her nose
Watchful black crows parade the cliff wall

Heidi, a puppy of thirteen
Soon to be fourteen
Where her light will always shine

Val Stephenson

Stolen Moment

Tread softly, for my dreams lie at your feet,
And in future time, perhaps our minds may meet,
And the darkest hours of day and night,
May rise to shine and put our world to rights.

And if my chance the winds of change may fall,
Without our hearing love's enchanted call,
Then thou shalt know that e'er I shall be true,
And will hold none sacred, saving you.

If life were fair, and chances sweet,
It would have been our destiny to meet,
When youth and innocence, assumes the way,
Which brings two people closer, day by day.

But if at night, you chance to dream,
Of meadows sweet and valleys green,
Imagine me, barefoot, happy, free,
Where age and time are no responsibility.

Please don't be sad, as I pass on my way,
Tomorrow, is yet, another day,
Enjoy your life, a life divine,
And in the next life, thou wilt be mine.

H M Jones

First Time

First glance, first look,
  first time, you're hooked.

First smile, first date,
  first time, it's fate.

First touch, first sigh,
  first time, you cry.

First love, first kiss,
  first time, what bliss.

Deanna L Dixon

My Saviour

Ode to my golden retriever
Who never fails to smile,
and pick me up when I feel down.
Who has not a care in the world,
and so sets me free
from this everyday cage,
which I often find myself in.
Who performs his magical spell
on all who care to meet him
and never gives up
on the promise of a long walk.
Oh, if life was as simple
perhaps I to would spend my days
lying in the long grass in the garden.
Just because he is always so happy to see me
makes me smile inside.
He is always loving
always forgiving,
and most importantly
knows how to make me smile.

S E Barnwell